B
CEZANNE

Mason, Anthony.

Cezanne.

$10.95

000029126
12/04/1997

DATE			

FAMOUS ARTISTS

CÉZANNE

The author, Antony Mason, is a freelance editor and author of many books for children.

Designer	Tessa Barwick
Editor	Jen Green
Picture research	Emma Krikler
Illustrators	Michaela Stewart
	Tessa Barwick

First edition for the United States, Canada, and the Philippines
published 1994 by Barron's Educational Series, Inc.

Designed and produced by
Aladdin Books Ltd
28 Percy Street
London W1P 9FF

First published in
Great Britain in 1993 by
Watts Books
96 Leonard Street
London EC2A 4RH

All inquiries should be addressed to:
Barron's Educational Series, Inc.
250 Wireless Boulevard
Hauppauge, New York 11788

Library of Congress Catalog Card No.: 94-14126

Mason, Anthony.
Cézanne / Anthony Mason.
p. cm.–(Famous artists)
"First published in Great Britain in 1993 by Watts Books"–T.p. verso
Includes index.
ISBN 0-8120-6459-3 (hardcover).–ISBN 0-8120-1293-3 (pbk.).
1. Cézanne, Paul. 1839-1906–Juvenile literature. 2. Painters France Biography–Juvenile
literature. [1. Cézanne, Paul, 1839-1906. 2. Artists. 3. Painting, French. 4. Art appreciation.]
I. Title. II. Series
ND553.C33M335   1994
759.4–dc20
[B]   94-14126
CIP
AC

International Standard Book No. 0-8120-6459-3 (hardcover)
0-8120-1293-3 (paperback)

Printed in Belgium
4567 4208 987654321

FAMOUS ARTISTS

CÉZANNE

ANTONY MASON

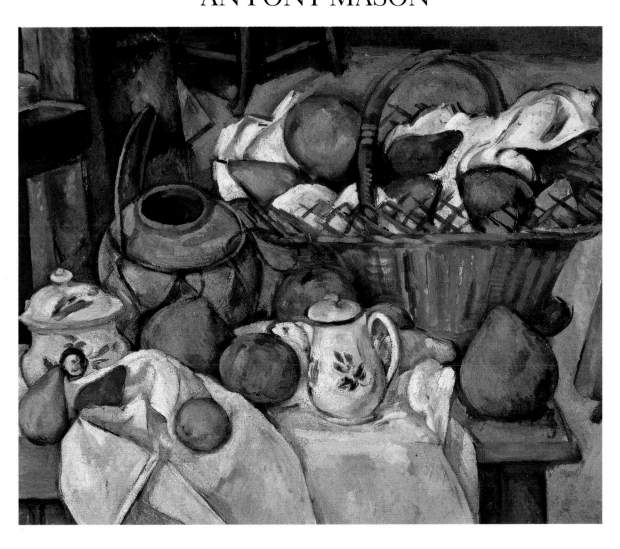

BARRON'S

CONTENTS

 The Bridge at Maincy near Melun, painted in 1879

INTRODUCTION

Paul Cézanne (1839-1906) lived in an exciting period of European painting. During the 1870s the Impressionist movement in art developed a new way of depicting the world. Cézanne worked alongside the Impressionists, but had other interests. He wanted to investigate the form, color, and structure of objects and how they could relate to each other in a painting. By his final years he was recognized as one of the most important painters of his time. He had a direct influence on the history of art in the twentieth century. This book explores Cézanne's development, from a self-taught youth in Paris to his final years in Aix-en-Provence. It traces his life and discusses the techniques he used to create his major works. You can try some of these techniques yourself. Below you can see how the book is organized.

Illustration of the artist's home or environment

The story of the artist's life

An enlargement of part of the painting

About the artist's work at the time

A feature on the artist's technique with practical projects

The size of the work is indicated by these symbols.

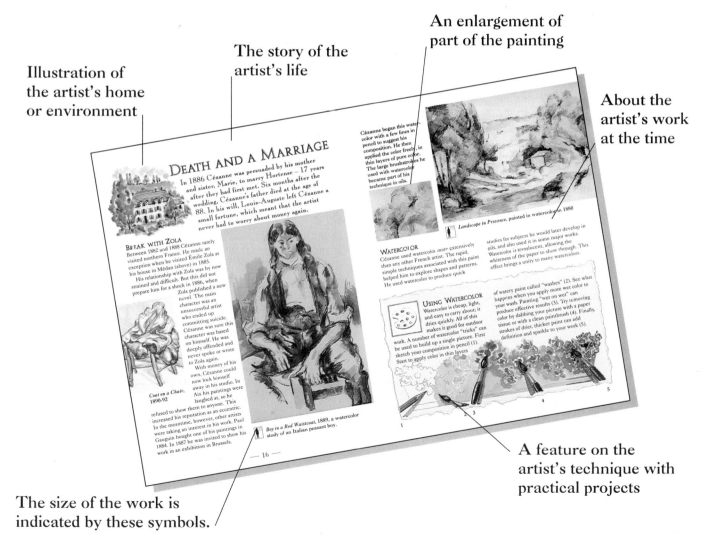

DEATH AND A MARRIAGE

In 1886 Cézanne was persuaded by his mother and sister, Marie, to marry Hortense – 17 years after they had first met. Six months after the wedding, Cézanne's father died at the age of 88. In his will, Louis-Auguste left Cézanne a small fortune, which meant that the artist never had to worry about money again.

BREAK WITH ZOLA
Between 1882 and 1888 Cézanne rarely visited northern France. He made an exception when he visited Émile Zola at his house in Médan (above) in 1885.
His relationship with Zola was by now strained and difficult. But this did not prepare him for a shock in 1886, when Zola published a new novel. The main character was an unsuccessful artist who ended up committing suicide. Cézanne was sure this character was based on himself. He was deeply offended and never spoke or wrote to Zola again.
With money of his own, Cézanne could now lock himself away in his studio. In Aix his paintings were laughed at, so he refused to show them to anyone. This increased his reputation as an eccentric. In the meantime, however, other artists were taking an interest in his work. Paul Gauguin bought one of his paintings in 1884. In 1887 he was invited to show his work in an exhibition in Brussels.

Coat on a Chair, 1890-92

Boy in a Red Waistcoat, 1889, a watercolor study of an Italian peasant boy.

Cézanne began this watercolor with a few lines in pencil to suggest his composition. He then applied the color freely, in thin layers of pure color. The large brushstrokes he used with watercolor became part of his technique in oils.

Landscape in Provence, painted in watercolor in 1880

WATERCOLOR
Cézanne used watercolor more extensively than any other French artist. The rapid, simple techniques associated with this paint helped him to explore shapes and patterns. He used watercolor to produce quick studies for subjects he would later develop in oils, and also used it in some major works. Watercolor is translucent, allowing the whiteness of the paper to show through. This effect brings a unity to many watercolors.

USING WATERCOLOR
Watercolor is cheap, light, and easy to carry about; it dries quickly. All of this makes it good for outdoor work. A number of watercolor "tricks" can be used to build up a single picture. First sketch your composition in pencil (1). Start to apply color in thin layers of watery paint called "washes" (2). See what happens when you apply more wet color to your wash. Painting "wet on wet" can produce effective results (3). Try removing color by dabbing your picture with a paper tissue or with a clean paintbrush (4). Finally, strokes of drier, thicker paint can add definition and sparkle to your work (5).

— 16 —

EARLY LIFE

Paul Cézanne was born in 1839 in the town of Aix-en-Provence, in the south of France. He was the oldest child in a wealthy family. His father, Louis-Auguste, was a merchant dealing in hats, who in 1848 set up the only bank in Aix. Paul's father hoped he would join the family business, but Paul showed more interest in art.

A HESITANT START

As a child, Paul Cézanne was strong, lively, and wild. He got along well with his sister, Marie, and his mother, Elisabeth, but his father was a hardened businessman who treated him strictly. Paul went to a local school in Aix. There he became close friends with Émile Zola (1840-1902), who was to become a well-known writer. Together they explored the countryside, sketched, and wrote poems. In 1859, when Paul was 20, his father bought an old manor house (above) outside Aix. It was called Jas de Bouffan and remained the family home for 40 years.

That year Paul went to law school in Aix. Émile Zola had gone to Paris, and Paul wanted to join him there and study art. After two frustrating years studying law, he was at last allowed to go to Paris.

In Paris he attended an informal kind of art school called the Atelier Suisse. But he soon began to doubt his ability. He gave up after five months and returned to Aix to work in his father's bank. But a year later he returned to Paris, and this time he stayed.

In this portrait painted about 1866, Cézanne gives a kindly impression of his father.

VIGOROUS YOUTH

Cézanne's early paintings show a crude energy. His subjects were often violent and nightmarish, and painted in dark colors. Although he soon improved his skills in drawing through dedicated practice, he was often frustrated by his inability to draw well. Instead, he used very thick layers of paint, often applied with a palette knife. This technique was used by one of his favorite artists, Gustave Courbet (1819-77). In his choice of ordinary subjects and his original techniques, Courbet questioned and challenged the old values of established painters in just the kind of way that Cézanne wanted to do.

Cézanne painted a number of portraits of his uncle. He worked quickly, applying the paint in layers so thick that it cracked. Usually, artists using oil paints smoothed one color into another.

Cézanne painted this portrait of his Uncle Dominic in a cotton cap in 1865.

PAINTING WITH A PALETTE KNIFE

To make an object like this boot look rounded and three-dimensional in a painting, you need to reproduce the effect of light falling on it. This can be done most accurately with a paintbrush. But you can create a similar effect by applying layers of paint with a palette knife. This rapid technique can give your picture a great sense of energy. Use a thick paint that will not run, such as acrylic or thick poster paint. Scoop up the paint on the palette knife (or any flexible knife) like jam from a jar, and smear it on. Try to keep the colors pure and unmixed.

Palette knife

Paintbrush

STUDYING IN PARIS

In Paris Cézanne worked hard, visiting galleries, particularly the Louvre (left) to sketch the paintings by great artists that hung there. He mixed with a young crowd of talented artists who were dissatisfied with current tastes in art and were searching for new ways to paint.

YOUNG ARTISTS

Among the artists Cézanne met in Paris were Edouard Manet, Camille Pissarro, Claude Monet, Auguste Renoir, and Edgar Degas. Within 30 years these men would be some of the most famous artists in Europe, but at this time they were virtually unknown.

In 1869, when he was 30, Cézanne met a 19-year-old artists' model named Hortense Fiquet, who became his girlfriend. In general he found it difficult to make friends. He was shy, awkward, and moody, and his manner often appeared rude.

Still Life with Black Clock, 1869-70, shows the calmer mood of Cézanne's new paintings.

The name *Jas de Bouffan* means "Habitation of the Winds." The house stood on beautiful grounds, which Cézanne painted often. He captured the dappled leaves with thick strokes of oil paint.

The avenue at Jas de Bouffan, painted about 1869.

LINKS WITH THE PAST

Throughout his painting career, Cézanne pursued his own vision. Compared to the other artists in his circle, he was virtually self-taught, and this gave him a different view of painting, which was original.

Despite this, Cézanne was convinced that he had to learn from Old Masters in order to create something new and lasting. He studied and copied works by famous artists throughout his life.

LEARNING FROM FAMOUS ARTISTS

For many centuries, artists have learned by studying the works of the great painters. Try this yourself. Find a good, large print of a painting you like in a book, or better still, visit a gallery and draw from a real painting. (You may have to ask the gallery's permission first.) Study the composition of the picture to see how all the elements are brought together. Look at the way the paint has been applied and how the artist has portrayed light and shadow. Now sketch the painting or a part that interests you.

IMPRESSIONISM

In July 1870 France began a war with Prussia, now part of Germany, and later that year Paris was besieged by Prussian armies. Cézanne managed to flee the city at the outbreak of the war, and traveled with Hortense to L'Estaque (left) on the south coast of France. Here he began to take an intense interest in landscape painting.

A SECRET LIFE

Cézanne left Paris for the south of France in the summer of 1870, before he could be called to serve in the French army. He was still a struggling artist whose work was not appreciated; critics thought it was crude and technically poor. Cézanne could not hope to live from his painting. However, he received an allowance from his father, half of which he gave to Hortense. He knew his father would be angry about this, so he did not tell him about Hortense. They traveled back to Paris when the war ended in 1871, and in the following January their son Paul was born. Cézanne did not tell his father about this either.

Later that year, they went to live outside Paris, first at Pontoise, where the painter Camille Pissarro had a home, and later at the nearby village of Auvers-sur-Oise. Cézanne had met Pissarro at the Atelier Suisse when he first went to Paris in 1861. At this time, four artists – Pissarro, Renoir, Monet, and Alfred Sisley – were developing a style of painting that later became known as "Impressionism." By using short, rapid brush-strokes and light colors, these artists aimed to capture the mood of scenes from everyday life as they changed from moment to moment, or the effect of light on a landscape at a particular time of day.

The Suicide's House, painted in 1873-74, shows the influence of Impressionist ideas.

SUNSHINE AND COLOR

The early 1870s were important years for Cézanne. He had traveled regularly to the south of France during his student days in Paris, but now he began to appreciate the light and color of the southern landscape. Like the Impressionists, he started to use lighter colors, as well as lighter brush strokes. His subject matter became less gloomy as he turned to landscapes, portraits, and still lifes. Hortense probably played an important part in the change. This relationship made his life more stable, although he never lost his reputation for odd behavior and outbursts of anger.

Compared to his earlier portraits, Cézanne now used a brighter, varied, and more daring range of colors. His brush-marks were also lighter, and the overall effect was more delicate and sensitive.

 Self-Portrait in a Cap, 1873-75, was one of many of Cézanne's portraits of himself.

IMPRESSIONIST ART

Create an Impressionist landscape by using the techniques of the Impressionists. Sketch your composition, but not in too much detail. Look at the colors of the scene in front of you and how light is affecting them; the same scene would look different at dawn, midday, and dusk. Study the subtle changes in tone in large areas of color like the sky. Represent these with flecks of paint of differing tones. Use light, bright colors.

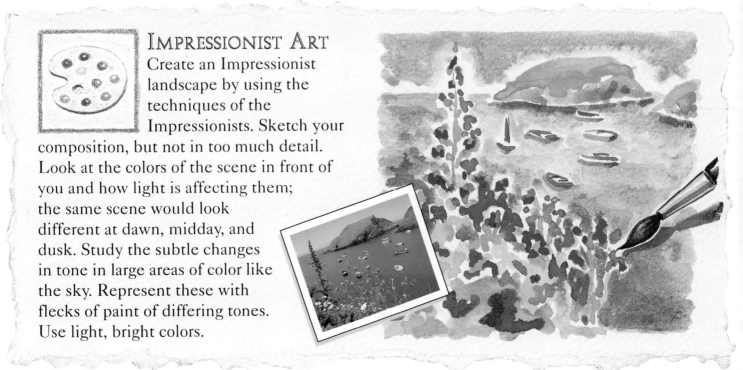

FINDING A STYLE

Despite his close contacts with Impressionism, Cézanne was not a true Impressionist. After 1877 he realized that he was not interested in capturing the mood of the moment, as the Impressionists were. Instead he wanted to explore the essential shapes and structures of things. The decision to follow his own path led to criticism and ridicule.

Madame Cézanne in a Red Armchair, painted in 1877. Cézanne has set Hortense against a block of vibrant red. The colors in the background are faintly echoed in the main figure.

MONEY PROBLEMS

Of all the painters he knew, only Pissarro had enough faith in Cézanne's talent – and enough patience with his awkwardness – to help him. Pissarro was ten years older than Cézanne and taught him a great deal as they painted together around Pontoise.

In 1872 Cézanne met Dr. Gachet, who had a house at Auvers (above). This kindly doctor encouraged Cézanne by buying several of his paintings. A supplier of painting materials named Julien Tanguy also helped him by taking his paintings in exchange for more oil paint.

Cézanne stayed in Auvers until 1874, then returned to Paris. That year he exhibited at the first Impressionist exhibition in Paris. The show was widely criticized. Cézanne's work was singled out for scornful remarks, but he sold one painting. Soon a collector called Victor Chocquet also began to buy his work.

After 1876 Cézanne returned regularly to L'Estaque. In 1878 his father learned about Hortense and the child, Paul. He was furious and cut Cézanne's allowance in half. Cézanne had to borrow money from his old friend, Émile Zola.

Post-Impressionism

Cézanne was beginning to look at the world in purely visual terms, attempting to arrange the shapes he saw in a satisfactory way. He is often called a "Post-Impressionist," because his work followed from Impressionism.

Émile Zola had become a successful author. He entertained many writers and artists at his large house at Médan. Cézanne went to visit him in 1879, but felt out of place even in the company of his old friend.

The Château of Médan stood on the river Seine close to Zola's house. This composition divides up horizontally into areas of sky, trees, houses, bank, and river. But the painting is unified by diagonal brushstrokes.

 Cézanne painted the Château of Médan during his visit with Zola.

THE SALONS

Every year an exhibition of paintings called the Salon took place in Paris. The Salons claimed to show the best in French art, but they were not adventurous; the judges chose paintings that demonstrated skillful technique and dignified subject matter. Cézanne and the Impressionists were consistently rejected. In 1863 a group of artists had become so annoyed by this that they set up the "Salon des Refusés," a show of rejected work.

LANDSCAPE ARTIST

After 1877 Cézanne no longer showed his work with the Impressionists. He felt his painting was moving in a different direction. Whereas the Impressionists used rapid brushstrokes to depict the fleeting play of light, Cézanne tended to use slabs of color, as seen below. Although he had moved away from Impressionist ideas, he still took pleasure in the company of other artists.

ARTIST COMPANIONS

For about a year, Cézanne lived with Hortense and their son Paul at Melun, a town to the south of Paris. In 1881 he returned to Pontoise to spend the summer painting with Pissarro. He also met Paul Gauguin, who was later to make a name for himself as a Post-Impressionist painter. In 1882 Cézanne returned to L'Estaque. Auguste Renoir came to visit him there, but caught pneumonia. Cézanne took Renoir back to his family home at Aix where, in the care of Cézanne's mother, he recovered.

Mountains in Provence, **painted in 1878-80**

Shapes of different elements in landscape, such as mountains, houses, and trees, echo one another in Cézanne's paintings. Here the quay in the top left corner echoes the line of the road below. The distant mountains have a bluish tone.

L'Estaque, 1882. The view of the bay was a favorite subject.

IN THE OPEN AIR

Like Pissarro and other Impressionists, Cézanne would walk out into the countryside to paint, with his materials strapped to his back. This was unusual at the time. By 1880 he had developed his own attitude about landscapes. He felt the Impressionist approach led to a lack of structure and was too lightweight. Instead he searched for ways to give landscape a grand quality, as the Old Masters had.

SHOWING DEPTH

When painting landscape a number of techniques can give your work a sense of depth, or distance. Colors are often more intense in the foreground nearest the viewer, and paler in the distance. Distant objects such as hills also often look bluish in tone. Objects that are closer appear to overlap those that are further away. Of course, you can see a lot more detail in the foreground than in the background. Be sure to reflect this in your work.

DEATH AND A MARRIAGE

In 1886 Cézanne was persuaded by his mother and sister, Marie, to marry Hortense – 17 years after they had first met. Six months after the wedding, Cézanne's father died at the age of 88. In his will, Louis-Auguste left Cézanne a small fortune, which meant that the artist never had to worry about money again.

BREAK WITH ZOLA

Between 1882 and 1888 Cézanne rarely visited northern France. He made an exception when he visited Émile Zola at his house in Médan (above) in 1885.

His relationship with Zola was by now strained and difficult. But this did not prepare him for a shock in 1886, when Zola published a new novel. The main character was an unsuccessful artist who ended up committing suicide. Cézanne was sure this character was based on himself. He was deeply offended and never spoke or wrote to Zola again.

With money of his own, Cézanne could now lock himself away in his studio. In Aix his paintings were laughed at, so he refused to show them to anyone. This increased his reputation as an eccentric. In the meantime, however, other artists were taking an interest in his work. Paul Gauguin bought one of his paintings in 1884. In 1887 he was invited to show his work in an exhibition in Brussels.

Coat on a Chair,
1890-92

 Boy in a Red Waistcoat, 1889, a watercolor study of an Italian peasant boy.

Cézanne began this water-color with a few lines in pencil to suggest his composition. He then applied the color freely, in thin layers of pure color. The large brushstrokes he used with watercolor became part of his technique in oils.

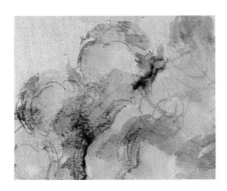

Landscape in Provence, painted in watercolor in 1880

WATERCOLOR

Cézanne used watercolor more extensively than any other French artist. The rapid, simple techniques associated with this paint helped him to explore shapes and patterns. He used watercolor to produce quick studies for subjects he would later develop in oils, and also used it in some major works. Watercolor is translucent, allowing the whiteness of the paper to show through. This effect brings a unity to many watercolors.

USING WATERCOLOR

Watercolor is cheap, light, and easy to carry about; it dries quickly. All of this makes it good for outdoor work. A number of watercolor "tricks" can be used to build up a single picture. First sketch your composition in pencil (1). Start to apply color in thin layers of watery paint called "washes" (2). See what happens when you apply more wet color to your wash. Painting "wet on wet" can produce effective results (3). Try removing color by dabbing your picture with a paper tissue or with a clean paintbrush (4). Finally, strokes of drier, thicker paint can add definition and sparkle to your work (5).

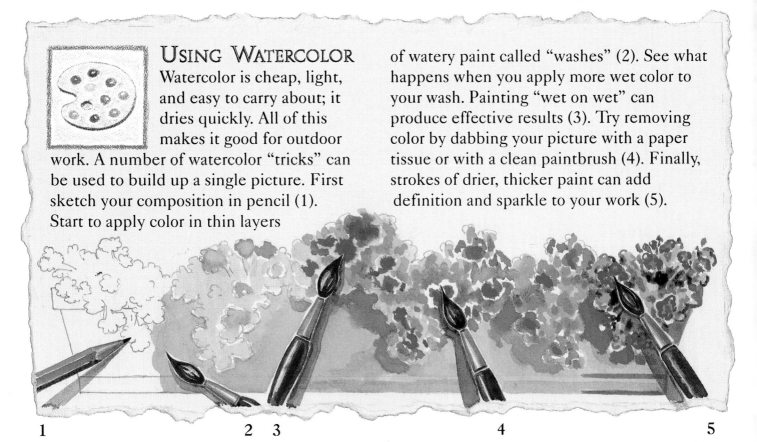

1   2   3   4   5

Separate Lives

In 1888 Cézanne returned to Paris and lived there for a year. After this he resumed the pattern of his earlier life, dividing his time between Paris and the south. In Paris he could keep up to date with developments in the art world; in the country he could work in his studio, or paint in the open air, without interruption.

A Widening Gulf

In 1890 Cézanne spent five months with his wife and son in Switzerland. After this Hortense spent most of her time in Paris. The relationship between Cézanne and his wife had become cool; Hortense was loyal but not devoted. She was never entirely convinced of her husband's talent and did not fully understand what he was trying to achieve. Cézanne, however, remained very attached to his son, Paul. The artist was becoming increasingly solitary. At about this time he began to suffer from diabetes, too much blood-sugar, which often left him feeling weak and tired.

The Card Players

Despite poor health, Cézanne worked hard, concentrating on certain themes. One of these was card players. Once he had discovered a theme that interested him, he would paint it over and over again, looking for the most satisfactory composition, or arrangement of his subject. The subject of card players appealed to him because it had been painted by the Old Masters, although usually with the intention of moralizing on the evils of gambling. Cézanne was more interested by the shapes of the figures grouped around a table, intent on their game. The subject involved ordinary people. Cézanne used local workers from Aix as models.

Man Smoking a Pipe, 1890-92. Cézanne used this sitter for the painting on page 19.

In his paintings of card players, Cézanne used quieter, more muted colors: red-browns, sepias, grays and yellow ochre. The cards themselves were not portrayed in detail.

The Card Players, 1892, is one of many versions of this subject.

VARIATIONS ON A THEME

Cézanne painted and sketched card players repeatedly between 1890 and 1894, trying to apply his ideas about shape and form to compositions involving human figures.

Early versions were complex, involving four or five figures gathered around a table. In later versions Cézanne simplified his composition, showing only two figures.

WAYS OF SEEING

Cézanne believed he was researching "ways of seeing," portraying a subject from different angles and sometimes in different materials, to put across the essence of his theme. Try the same approach yourself. Make different versions of a subject, such as playing cards. Show your subject from various angles and use different materials, such as paint, colored pencils, and crayons. Try different styles of coloring, too, experimenting with techniques you haven't used before. When you have finished, study the results. Which version do you like best? Why?

First Successes

Cézanne continued to divide his time between Paris and Aix, where he looked after his aging mother with great tenderness. At Jas de Bouffan he found the peace he needed to concentrate on landscapes, still lifes, and figure drawing. At last his perseverance was beginning to pay off, for by the mid-1890s his paintings started to sell at good prices.

Artists' Acclaim

In 1895 Cézanne had his first exhibition on his own, which was organized by the art dealer Ambroise Vollard in Paris. It marked a turning point in his career. The painters Monet, Renoir, Pissarro, and Degas all expressed their admiration for his work. Pissarro was particularly enthusiastic, praising Cézanne's sense of color: "He is a first-class painter of astonishing subtlety, truth, and classicism." The work was praised by critics too: "Today it has suddenly been discovered that Zola's friend, the mysterious man from Provence, the painter sly and uncivilized, is a great man," one critic reported.

Still Life

A still life is a painting of everyday objects. It was one of Cézanne's favorite subjects, and he would spend a long time setting up his composition, as an onlooker had observed: "Cézanne arranged the fruits, contrasting the tones one against the other, the greens against the reds, the yellows against the blues, tipping, turning, balancing the fruits as he wanted them to be, using coins of one or two sous for the purpose. One guessed it was a feast for the eye to him."

Still Life with Plaster Cupid is a complex composition. Cézanne worked on it over three years (1892-95).

Cézanne achieved a feeling of harmony by making colors and shapes in different areas of the picture interact with one another. Here the color and shape of the fruit is echoed in the painted screen behind.

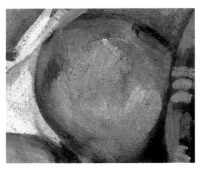

Kitchen Still Life, 1888-90

SLOW PROGRESS

Cézanne painted slowly. Often the fruit had shriveled or the flowers withered long before he had finished. He returned to his canvases repeatedly, amending them little by little.

As a result, many of his paintings took years to complete. He signed very few, suggesting that he was not satisfied with most and did not consider them finished.

SETTING UP A STILL LIFE

Still lifes are good practice for working on composition. Take time to arrange your objects carefully. Try them out in different positions until you reach the arrangement you find balanced and pleasing.

Now study the objects closely, noting color, shape, and texture. Try doing two versions of the same composition. In one version you could try to convey how fruit looks and feels. In the other you could work in a more abstract way to convey echoes and contrasts in shape and color.

THE PRICE OF FAME

After the exhibition organized by Ambroise Vollard, Cézanne's work began to be praised by a number of influential critics. However, the artist was not happy about the attention he received as a result. "I thought that one could do good painting without attracting attention to one's private life," he wrote.

DEATH OF ELISABETH

In 1897 Cézanne's mother died. This affected him far more than his father's death 11 years earlier. He withdrew from his wife and friends, retreating into his own world, and concentrated obsessively on painting. His own health was causing him increasing concern. His sister, Marie, took over the running of the family home, Jas de Bouffan.

PORTRAITS

During the 1890s Cézanne painted a number of portraits of his family and friends, as well as self-portraits. It was not easy to sit for him; he worked extremely slowly, making his subjects sit in awkward positions for long hours. Ambroise Vollard posed for him and was urged to sit absolutely still, "like an apple." After 115 sittings the painting was still not complete, the artist being unsure what tone to use to paint the art dealer's hand. "Don't you see, Monsieur Vollard," Cézanne explained, "if I put something there by guesswork, I might have to paint the whole canvas over, starting from that point?" "The prospect made me tremble," Vollard commented.

This self-portrait in watercolor was painted in 1895, when Cézanne was 56. It shows the artist looking anxious and tired.

 Cézanne painted this portrait of a peasant between 1895 and 1900.

CONTRASTING COLORS

In painting portraits Cézanne employed many of the same techniques that he had used in his landscapes and still lifes, such as blocks of color and slanting brushstrokes. He also used contrasting colors – greens and reds, or blues and oranges. Such colors are called *complementary* colors. They intensify one another when placed side by side, and in Cézanne's work they add drama.

The subject of working people continued to interest Cézanne. In 1895 he began a painting of a farm worker sitting in front of a decorative screen portraying a fanciful scene from rural life.

The screen was one Cézanne and Zola had painted in their youth at Jas de Bouffan. Perhaps the farmer's wistful expression reflects the artist's own sadness at the loss of his boyhood friend.

PAINTING PORTRAITS

Sketch in the basic shapes first, making sure the head sits correctly on the shoulders. Sketch in lines for the eyes, nose, and mouth, to position them correctly before working on details. Portrait artists often start with the figure and paint in the background later. But Cézanne frequently gave the background as much importance as his subject. Try working on the background as you paint the portrait. This will help to balance colors in your picture and create depth.

HOMAGE TO CÉZANNE

In 1898 Vollard organized another exhibition for Cézanne, but in the following years the artist stayed almost permanently at Aix. Although his paintings were now selling well, he continued to prefer the solitude of his beloved Provence. "I am deeply in love with the landscape of my country," he wrote.

EXHIBITIONS

In 1899 and 1900 Cézanne's paintings were exhibited at the Salon des Indépendants, and in 1900 at the Centenary Exhibition in Paris. This was a great triumph for a painter who had been so widely criticized for so long. His work was now being sought by galleries and collectors. In 1900 Maurice Denis painted *Homage to Cézanne* – a group portrait of contemporary artists standing around one of Cézanne's still lifes. It demonstrated that many young artists saw Cézanne as a major influence in modern art.

Apples, Bottles and Chairback, a watercolor painted between 1902 and 1906

ABANDONING REALISM

Young artists admired Cézanne because his work represented a new approach to art. He was not trying to portray reality – the world as it is, as even the Impressionists had done. Rather, he used paint for the pleasure of the designs he could create from it. In paintings such as *The Big Trees*, Cézanne created a kind of mosaic, treating all shapes in the foreground and background individually. He simplified the world, yet produced something very satisfying from it. No one had tried to paint like this before. Cézanne's work opened up the possibility of creative freedom.

Cézanne's landscapes were now more abstract. He was as interested in the background – in the shapes between objects – as in the objects themselves. He was one of the first to emphasize what is now called "negative space."

The Big Trees, 1904, reflects the abstract nature of Cézanne's work at this time.

NEGATIVE SPACE

Painting "negative space" provides a new way of seeing shapes, and surprisingly, can help you to draw much more accurately. Try painting the branches of a tree. Now try the same subject again, focusing on the shape of the spaces between the branches, rather than the branches themselves. The effect is no longer just a tree, but something new and original. The same technique can provide a fresh approach to still lifes, figure drawing, and portraits, too.

THE RECLUSE

On Cézanne's mother's death, the wealth that had been amassed by his father was divided equally between the artist and his sisters. In 1899 they decided to sell Jas de Bouffan. Cézanne moved into a small flat in Aix, where a housekeeper looked after him. Meanwhile, he had a studio built on the outskirts of the town.

ALONE WITH HIS WORK

In 1902 Cézanne began to use his new studio, walking there each day from his flat. In the autumn of 1904 a whole room was devoted to his work at the Salon in Paris, but he was no longer interested in acclaim. After years of struggle, acknowledgment came too late to give him much pleasure.

In 1902 news reached Cézanne of the death of his former friend Zola. He burst into tears and shut himself away in his studio. So few people actually saw him now that he had become a legend. Estranged from his wife, Hortense, his only love was painting, toward which he directed all his energy.

 The Great Bathers, which Cézanne worked on for eight years, from 1898 to 1906

In the 1870s Cézanne had begun a series of paintings depicting nude bathers in a landscape, a theme that occupied him increasingly in his later years. He struggled to achieve the power and timelessness he admired in the work of the Old Masters. On the left you can see an early version of the same subject.

Cézanne painted bathers throughout his career.

FIGURES IN A LANDSCAPE

When painting his series of bathers in Aix, Cézanne could not use female models. This would have been considered shocking in the quiet provincial city. He told a collector, "An old (male) invalid poses for all these women."

He had continued to copy the work of great artists all his life. He made many studies of paintings and drawings of the human figure by artists he admired, including Rubens and Michelangelo. For Cézanne the subject was a challenge to make the figures fit harmoniously with the shapes of trees and clouds. These paintings were a major influence on a new generation of artists, including Pablo Picasso (1881-1973).

Cézanne wrote: "Drawing and outline are not distinct, since everything has color. By the very act of painting, one draws."

DRAWING WITH PAINT

Most of us are taught to paint first of all by coloring in pictures, carefully keeping the colors within the lines. But as much of Cézanne's work shows, you can create shapes by color alone. Try this out for yourself by painting a subject such as this sailboat without drawing any outline first. You can achieve a similar effect with crayons, as shown here.

FINAL YEARS

In his last years, Cézanne continued to paint his favorite subjects — still lifes, portraits, the bathers, and the view of Mont Sainte-Victoire, a rocky hill to the east of Aix. He suffered increasingly with diabetes. "I am old and ill, but have sworn to die painting," he wrote. Now in his 60s, Cézanne still kept to his customary pattern of work.

REGULAR ROUTINE

Cézanne would rise early, at five A.M. in summer to avoid the heat. His mornings were spent in the studio; in the afternoon he often sent for a carriage to take him into the countryside. He disliked spectators watching him, so would ask the driver to take him to a remote spot where he could paint undisturbed. He loved the late afternoon, when the air became crystal clear as the heat of the day lessened.

Mont Sainte-Victoire, painted about 1885

Mont Sainte-Victoire, painted between 1904 and 1906

MOUNTAIN OF VICTORY

The mountain of Sainte-Victoire could be seen from the grounds of Cézanne's family home at Aix, and from the hill above his studio. He had painted it throughout much of his life, and in his last years became almost obsessed by it. In early versions (above) the mountain was often framed by trees. In later versions (left) it stood alone, rising majestically from the plain. These final works show the extent of Cézanne's development and how far he had moved away from Impressionism and Realism.

Cézanne aimed to "treat nature in terms of the cylinder, the sphere, the cone." Landscape was now represented by blocks of color. This influenced the Cubists, who revolutionized art in the early twentieth century.

 Bend in the Road, 1900-1906

FATHER OF MODERN ART

In October 1906 Cézanne was caught in a storm when out painting, and fell ill with a chill. He died a few days later, at the age of 67, and was buried in his native town of Aix.

His later works broke new ground in painting; they were semi-abstract, although their subject was still clear. They were to influence many later movements in art. In the early twentieth century, the Cubists broke the world up into geometric shapes. After 1905, the Expressionists painted with vivid color, charged with emotion. With the arrival of abstract art in the 1920s, artists created paintings out of shape and pattern alone. All these trends could be said to originate in the work of Cézanne. This is why he is called "the father of modern art."

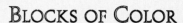

BLOCKS OF COLOR
The Cubists broke down subjects into shapes such as cubes and squares. They struggled to represent three-dimensional reality by showing different views of their subject within a single image. You could take this further by representing landscape with simple shapes. Mountains might become pyramids, and houses cubes. Does the painting look like the original, or have you created something new?

CHRONOLOGY OF CÉZANNE'S LIFE

1839 Born in Aix-en-Provence, in the south of France.

1852 (-58) Attended school in Aix, where he met Émile Zola.

1861 Abandoned his law studies in Aix to attend the Atelier Suisse, an art school in Paris.

1862 Met Pissarro, Renoir, Monet, Sisley, and other artists of the Impressionists' circle. For most of the rest of his life he divided his time between Aix and Paris.

1869 Met Hortense Fiquet, who later became his wife.

1870 Left Paris with Hortense to live in L'Estaque, in the south of France.

1872 Birth of their son, Paul. Moved near to Pontoise, northern France, where he painted with Pissarro.

1874 Took part in the first Impressionist exhibition.

1878 His father discovered the existence of Hortense and their child, and cut Cézanne's allowance in half.

1886 Married Hortense. His father died and left him a large sum of money. Cézanne was offended by Zola's novel about an artist.

1895 First exhibition on his own, organized by Ambroise Vollard. Growing appreciation and sales of his work. Cézanne led an increasingly lonely and isolated life.

1897 Death of Cézanne's mother.

1899 Jas de Bouffan sold.

1904 A room at the Paris Salon was devoted to Cézanne; he made his last visit to Paris.

1906 Died at Aix after being caught in a rainstorm.

A BRIEF HISTORY OF ART

The world's earliest works of art are figurines dating from 30,000 B.C. Cave art developed from 16,000 B.C. In the Classical Age (500-400 B.C.) sculpture flourished in Ancient Greece.

The Renaissance period began in Italy in the 1300s and reached its height in the sixteenth century. Famous Italian artists include Giotto (ca.1266-1337), Leonardo da Vinci (1452-1519), Michelangelo Buonarroti (1475-1564), and Titian (ca.1487-1576).

In Europe during the fifteenth and sixteenth centuries Hieronymus Bosch (active 1480-1516), Albrecht Dürer (1471-1528), Pieter Breughel the Elder (1525-69), and El Greco (1541-1614) produced great art. Artists of the Baroque period include Peter Paul Rubens (1577-1640) and Rembrandt van Rijn (1606-69).

During the Romantic movement English artists J.M.W. Turner (1775-1851) and John Constable (1776-1837) produced wonderful landscapes. Francisco Goya (1746-1828) was a great Spanish portrait artist.

Impressionism began in France in the 1870s. Artists include Claude Monet (1840-1926), Camille Pissarro (1830-1903), and Edgar Degas (1834-1917). Post-Impressionists include **Paul Cézanne** (1839-1906), Paul Gauguin (1848-1903), and Vincent van Gogh (1853-90).

The twentieth century has seen many movements in art. Piet Mondrian (1872-1944) painted in the Cubist tradition, Salvador Dali (1904-89) in the Surrealist. Pablo Picasso (1881-1973) was a prolific Spanish painter. More recently Jackson Pollock (1912-56) and David Hockney (1937-) have achieved fame.

MUSEUMS AND GALLERIES

The following museums and galleries have examples of Cézanne's work, but much of it is in private collections.

The Louvre, Paris, France

Musée d'Orsay, Paris, France

National Gallery, London, England

Tate Gallery, London, England

Courtauld Institute, London, England

National Gallery of Scotland

National Gallery, Washington DC, USA

Museum of Modern Art, New York, USA

Museum of Fine Arts, Boston, USA

Art Institute, Chicago, USA

Philadelphia Museum of Art, USA

Barnes Foundation, Merion, Pennsylvania, USA

Hermitage, St. Petersburg, Russia

Puskin Museum, Moscow, Russia

GLOSSARY

Composition All paintings contain elements that have been selected and positioned by the artist. The way in which these elements are arranged is called the composition.

Impressionism The Impressionist painters attempted to evoke the light and mood of a scene or landscape by using bright colors and small, rapid brushstrokes. The term *Impressionist* was invented in 1874, when an art critic used it to poke fun at the work of artists such as Monet, Sisley, Pissarro, Renoir, and Cézanne. The artists liked the word and referred to their style as Impressionism.

Perspective Since the fifteenth century, artists have used various ways to convey a sense of distance in their paintings. As a general rule, objects appear smaller and lighter in color the further away they are.

Post-Impressionism Several artists of the late nineteenth century, whose work followed closely from that of the Impressionists, are known as Post-Impressionists. They include Cézanne, Vincent van Gogh, and Paul Gauguin.

Realism Many artists have tried to portray the real world, as they saw it – not an idealized world, or a vision of the past. This approach is called "realism."

Tone Shades of color are sometimes referred to as tones. This can be a useful term, as sometimes the word shade can be confused with shadow.

Wash Watercolor can be applied in a very thin, watery layer, which is allowed to soak evenly into the paper, often as a background. This is known as a wash.

INDEX

INDEX OF PICTURES

Special thanks to: The Bridgeman Art Library. Giraudon/Bridgeman Art Library. Courtauld Institute Galleries, London (Courtauld Collection). Walter Feilchenfeldt, The Feilchenfeldt Collection, Zurich. National Gallery of Art, Washington. Museum of Fine Arts, Boston. National Gallery of Scotland. Tate Gallery, London. Hulton Deutsch, London. Roger Vlitos. The publishers have made every effort to contact all the relevant copyright holders and apologize for any omissions that may have inadvertently been made.